A Year of

YOU

& ME

A Journal of **365** Questions for
Couples to Spark Love and Connection

NADIA HAYES

CASTLE POINT BOOKS
NEW YORK

CONTENTS

DEAR COUPLE,

Let your love flow and have fun expressing what makes your relationship unique! With 365 insightful questions to discuss while curled up on the couch or enjoying your morning coffee, you'll never be short on meaningful conversation. Journey together through the daily prompts of *A Year of You & Me*, and add your answers next to each other on the page. At the end of the year, you'll have stellar communication skills, a happier and healthier relationship, and a time capsule to cherish forever.

Whether you've just met, are entering a new phase together, or have been married for years, get ready for the laughter, bonding, and quality time that *A Year of You & Me* will bring. Let it inspire you to make time for each other every day and strengthen your connection. Put your relationship first and enjoy a couple's adventure that lasts the whole year.

OUR OPENING ACT

day 1

Describe how we met.

_____

_____

. . . .

_____

_____

day 2

**What was your first impression of me?
How accurate is it now?**

_____

_____

. . . .

_____

_____

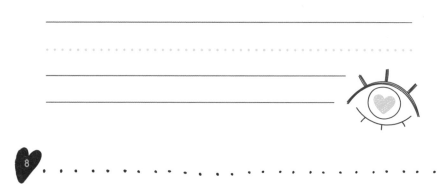

day **3**

Do you believe in fate?

☐ ☐ YES

☐ ☐ NO

☐ ☐ MAYBE

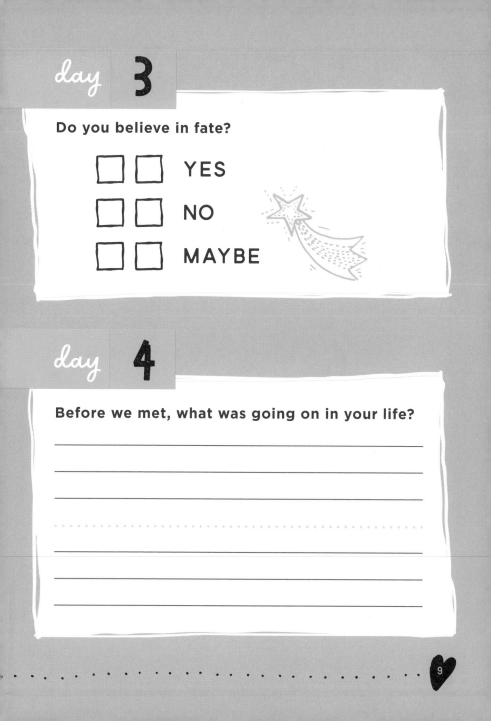

day **4**

Before we met, what was going on in your life?

_____

_____

_____

. . . .

_____

_____

_____

day 5

What changed after we met?

_____

_____

· ·

_____

_____

day 6

What do you remember most from our first date?

_____

_____

_____

· ·

_____

_____

_____

day 7

Who did you talk to about me? What did you say?

_____

_____

_____

· ·

_____

_____

_____

day 8

What makes you laugh when you think back to our early days?

_____

_____

_____

· ·

_____

_____

_____

day 9

What were you glad we had in common?

_____

_____

_____

. . . .

_____

_____

_____

day 10

What did you find unique or intriguing about me?

_____

_____

_____

. . . .

_____

_____

_____

day 11

What attracted you to me?

_____

_____

_____

. . . .

_____

_____

_____

day 12

What did you think of my family when you first met them?

_____

_____

. . . .

_____

_____

day 13

What did you think of my friends when you first met them?

_____

_____

. . . .

_____

_____

day 14

How nervous were you to introduce me to your inner circle? Explain.

_____

_____

. . . .

_____

_____

day 15

How was I your type (or not your type)?

_____
_____
_____
. . . .
_____
_____
_____

day 16

Describe a romantic moment from when we first started dating.

_____
_____
_____
. . . .
_____
_____
_____

day 17

What was the first fight you remember us having? How did we resolve it?

_____

_____

_____

· ·

_____

_____

_____

day 18

When did you know that we were going to stay together?

_____

_____

· ·

_____

_____

day 19

Who said *I love you* first? How did that feel?

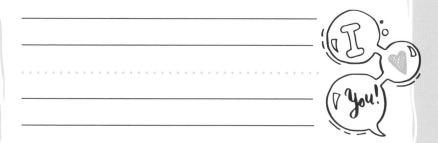

_____

_____

. . . .

_____

_____

day 20

What were you excited for us to do together?

_____

_____

_____

. . . .

_____

_____

_____

day 21

What early milestone meant the most to you?

_____

_____

. . . .

_____

_____

day 22

What information (or side of you) did you hold back at first?

_____

_____

_____

. . . .

_____

_____

_____

day 23

How long was it before you trusted me completely?

_____

_____

_____

. . . .

_____

_____

_____

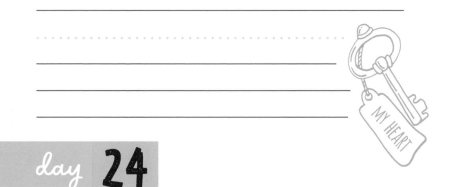

day 24

What were the first things we bonded over?

_____

_____

_____

. . . .

_____

_____

_____

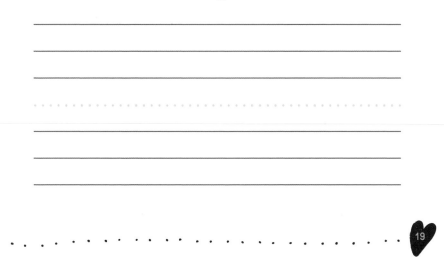

day 25

Where was our first vacation together, and how would you describe it?

_____

_____

_____

· ·

_____

_____

_____

day 26

When we met, what were you looking for in a relationship?

_____

_____

· ·

_____

_____

day 27

What pleasantly surprised you about me?

_____

_____

_____

_____

· ·

_____

_____

_____

day 28

What hopes did you have for us at the beginning of our relationship?

_____

_____

· ·

_____

_____

day 29

What helped us get to know each other?

_____
_____
_____
. . . .
_____
_____
_____

day 30

What side of you did I bring out?

_____
_____
. . . .
_____
_____

day 31

How would you describe our early chemistry?

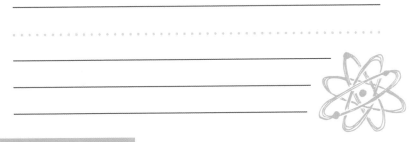

day 32

A memento I saved from those early days is:

Our initial connection was based on:

☐ ☐ **PHYSICAL ATTRACTION**

☐ ☐ **EASY CONVERSATION**

☐ ☐ **SHARED INTERESTS**

☐ ☐ **SOLID FRIENDSHIP**

☐ ☐ **OTHER:** _____

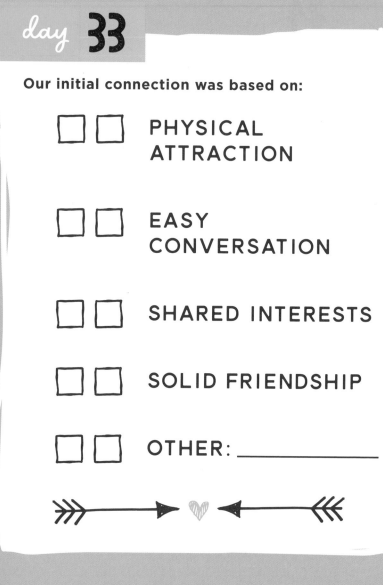

day 34

What did you like most about my physical appearance?

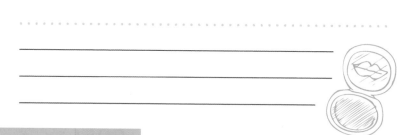

day 35

What did you like most about my personality?

day 36

In the beginning, our relationship moved:

☐ ☐ LIKE A BULLET TRAIN—
WE NEVER LOOKED BACK

☐ ☐ LIKE A LONG-DISTANCE RUNNER—
WE PACED OURSELVES

☐ ☐ LIKE A TURTLE—
WE WERE CAUTIOUS AND/OR BUSY

day 37

If you had a time machine, what moment
in our relationship would you return to?

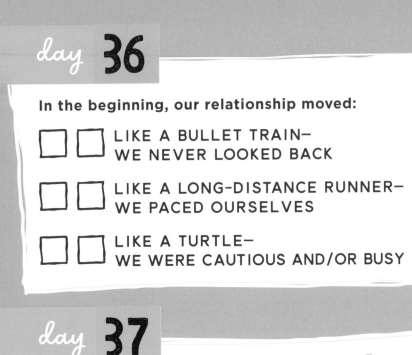

_____

_____

_____

. . . .

_____

_____

_____

YOUR LOVE *is* LIKE...

day 38

If I were to compare you to something in nature, it would be...

_____

_____

_____

_____

day 39

When I look into your eyes, I feel...

_____

_____

_____

_____

day **40**

Something irresistible about you is...

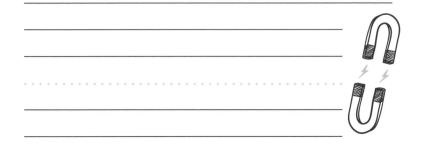

_____

_____

_____

. . . .

_____

_____

_____

day **41**

Something new you've brought into my life is . . .

_____

_____

_____

. . . .

_____

_____

_____

With you by my side, I'm more
(check all that apply):

☐ ☐ TRUSTING

☐ ☐ MYSELF

☐ ☐ OPEN-MINDED

☐ ☐ MATURE

☐ ☐ POSITIVE

☐ ☐ CONFIDENT

☐ ☐ OTHER:

_____

day 43

The song that best describes our love is...

_____

_____

_____

· ·

_____

_____

_____

day 44

Without you in my life, I'd be...

_____

_____

· ·

_____

_____

day 45

Sacrifices we've been happy to make for each other are...

_____

_____

_____

. . . .

_____

_____

_____

day 46

The way you look at me makes me feel...

_____

_____

_____

. . . .

_____

_____

_____

day 47

You're the only one who can...

_____

_____

_____

· ·

_____

_____

_____

day 48

I never knew a relationship could be so...

_____

_____

_____

· ·

_____

_____

_____

day 49

We go together like...

_____

_____

_____

· ·

_____

_____

_____

day 50

I know we're a good match because...

_____

_____

· ·

_____

_____

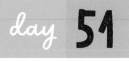

day **51**

We're at our best when we're...

_____
_____
_____
. . . .
_____
_____
_____

day **52**

**The movie that makes me think
of our relationship is...**

_____
_____
. . . .
_____
_____

day 53

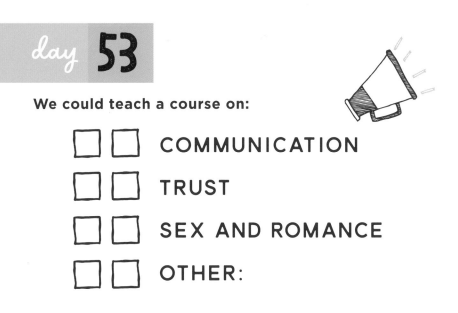

We could teach a course on:

☐ ☐ COMMUNICATION

☐ ☐ TRUST

☐ ☐ SEX AND ROMANCE

☐ ☐ OTHER:

_____

day 54

Something positive others have
said about our relationship is...

_____

_____

_____

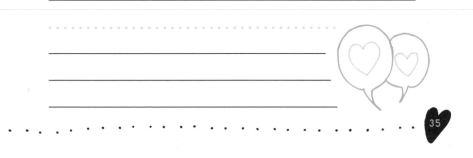

_____

_____

_____

day 55

I'm always amazed by your...

_____

_____

_____

· · · · · · · · · · · · · · · · · · ·

_____

_____

_____

day 56

**If I could describe our love in a line
of poetry, it would be this:**

_____

_____

_____

· · · · · · · · · · · · · · · · · · ·

_____

_____

_____

day 57

You have always believed in me. Remember when...

_____
_____
_____
. . . .
_____
_____
_____

day 58

I have always believed in you. Remember when...

_____
_____
. . . .
_____
_____

 day **59**

If today was our last day on Earth, we should spend it...

_____

_____

. . . .

_____

_____

 day **60**

My heart skips a beat when you...

_____

_____

_____

. . . .

_____

_____

_____

day 61

Your love gives me the strength to...

_____
_____
_____
. . . .
_____
_____
_____

day 62

Sometimes I look at you and think...

_____
_____
_____
. . . .
_____

day 63

Our first kiss was like...

_____

_____

. . . .

_____

_____

day 64

I love when you are feeling flirtatious and you...

_____

_____

_____

. . . .

_____

_____

_____

day 65

Who underestimates our relationship, and how have we proved them wrong?

_____

_____

· ·

_____

_____

day 66

What's the best way to make up after a fight?

_____

_____

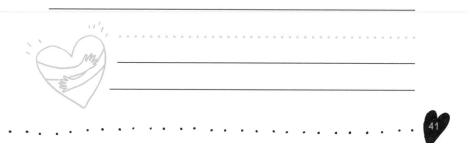

· ·

_____

_____

day 67

What reality show or game show do we have the best shot at winning?

_____

_____

· ·

_____

_____

day 68

If you were to guess, what would you say I'm thinking about right now?

_____

_____

_____

· ·

_____

_____

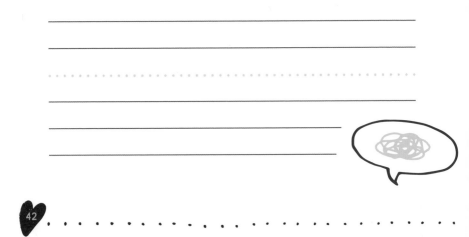

day 69

Which of the following are we most likely to fight about?

- ☐ ☐ FAMILY
- ☐ ☐ MONEY
- ☐ ☐ POLITICS
- ☐ ☐ HOUSEWORK
- ☐ ☐ OUR SOCIAL CALENDAR
- ☐ ☐ OTHER: _____
  _____

day 70

How could we resolve that topic or make peace?

_____

_____

_____

_____

What couple do you sometimes compare us to?

_____

_____

_____

. . . .

_____

_____

_____

What is a deal breaker for you?

_____

_____

. . . .

_____

_____

day 73

On a scale of 1 to 10, how independent are you?

_____

_____

_____

· ·

_____

_____

_____

day 74

What would you do for love?
What wouldn't you do?

_____

_____

_____

· ·

_____

_____

_____

day 75

What do you have a difficult time communicating? What's easy to say?

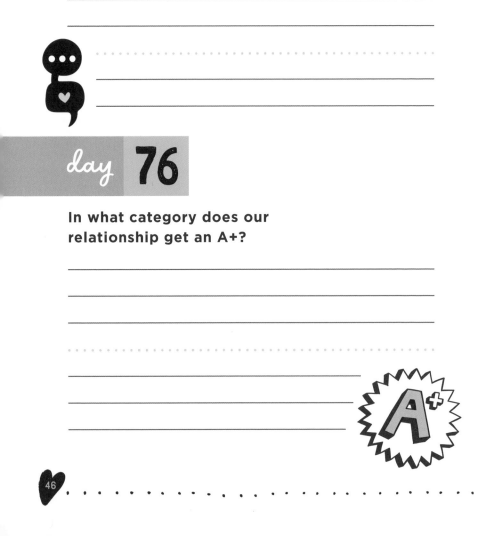

day 76

In what category does our relationship get an A+?

day 77

I promise you I'll always...

· ·

---

day 78

Something I'd like to say to your boss is:

· ·

day 79

Our relationship grew even stronger when...

_____

_____

_____

. . . .

_____

_____

_____

day 80

I'm proud of the way we've...

_____

_____

. . . .

_____

_____

day 81

A time when you stood up for me was...

_____

_____

_____

· ·

_____

_____

_____

day 82

What puts the most stress on our relationship? How can we lessen it?

_____

_____

_____

· ·

_____

_____

_____

day 83

What can we do to make our relationship even stronger?

_____

_____

_____

· ·

_____

_____

_____

day 84

How jealous would you say you are?

_____

_____

_____

· ·

_____

_____

_____

day 85

How much P.D.A. is too much?

day 86

What charity work do you see us getting involved in?

 **day 87**

What makes us unstoppable?

_____
_____
_____
. . . .
_____
_____
_____

 **day 88**

How do we make each other better?

_____
_____
. . . .
_____
_____
_____

FANNING *the* FLAMES

day 89

How would you describe our sex life?

☐ ☐ LEGENDARY

☐ ☐ SATISFYING

☐ ☐ IN NEED OF A
JUMP START

day 90

What's the best way to keep passion
alive in a relationship?

_____

_____

. . . .

_____

_____

day 91

When are you most attracted to me?

_____

_____

_____

. . . .

_____

_____

_____

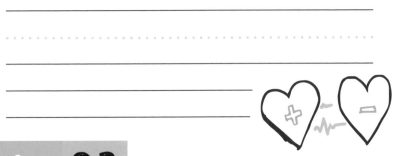

day 92

Who is more affectionate? Give an example.

_____

_____

_____

. . . .

_____

_____

_____

day 93

What makes a kiss perfect?

_____

_____

_____

· ·

_____

_____

day 94

What makes you feel closer to me?

_____

_____

· ·

_____

_____

day 95

When was your libido off the charts?

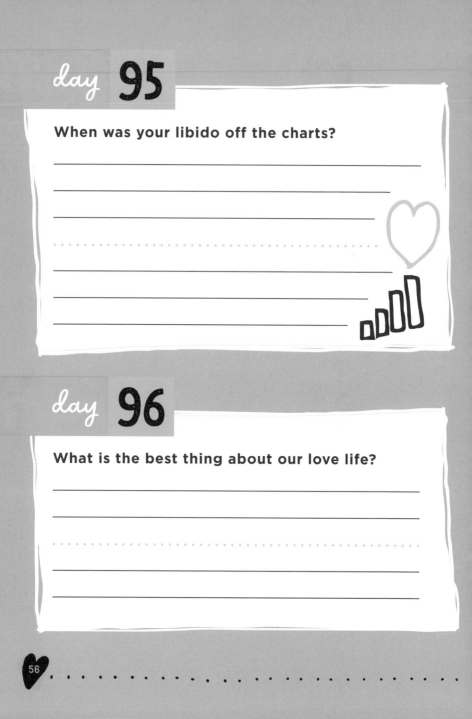

_____

_____

_____

· ·

_____

_____

_____

day 96

What is the best thing about our love life?

_____

_____

· ·

_____

_____

 **day 97**

What healthy adjustments have we made to our love life?

_____

_____

. . . .

_____

_____

 **day 98**

What part(s) of your body are you most proud of?

_____

_____

_____

. . . .

_____

_____

day **99**

**What part of your body are you
most self-conscious about?**

_____

_____

_____

· ·

_____

_____

_____

day **100**

Here's why I love that part of your body:

_____

_____

_____

· ·

_____

_____

_____

day 101

What outfit of mine do you find most attractive?

day 102

What is the sexiest thing I could say to you right now?

day **103**

How frequently do you think we should have sex?

_____

_____

. . . .

_____

_____

day **104**

What part of your body do you
enjoy having massaged most?

☐ ☐ FEET   ☐ ☐ OTHER:

☐ ☐ LEGS   _____

☐ ☐ BACK   _____

☐ ☐ NECK AND _____
      SHOULDERS _____

If you were to write a manual to your body, what chapter would you want me to read first?

_____

_____

_____

· ·

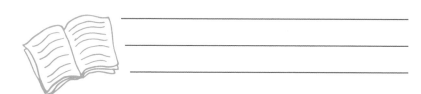

_____

_____

_____

How would you rate yourself as a kisser?

☐ ☐ GOLD MEDAL

☐ ☐ SILVER MEDAL

☐ ☐ BRONZE MEDAL

☐ ☐ I DON'T KISS AND TELL.

How would you rate yourself in bed?

☐ ☐ I SHOULD WRITE A BOOK.

☐ ☐ I'VE GOT MOVES.

☐ ☐ NO ONE'S EVER COMPLAINED.

☐ ☐ I NEED MORE PRACTICE.

day 108

**What turn-ons do you have that
I might not know about?**

_____

_____

_____

· ·

_____

_____

_____

day 109

What do you fantasize about?

_____

_____

_____

· ·

_____

_____

_____

 day **110**

What is your favorite thing to do after sex?

_____

_____

_____

· ·

_____

_____

_____

  day **111**

What celebrity do you think I most resemble?

_____

_____

_____

· ·

_____

_____

_____

 64

day 112

What is something new you'd like us to try?

_____
_____
_____
. . . .
_____
_____
_____

day 113

What is the best way to add romance to a day?

_____
_____
. . . .
_____
_____

day 114

How great a role does sex play in our relationship?

_____

_____

· ·

_____

_____

day 115

How has our physical connection developed over time?

_____

_____

· ·

_____

_____

day 116

List a few things you love about my body.

_____

_____

_____

· ·

_____

_____

_____

day 117

**The cutest thing about you when
you first wake up is...**

_____

_____

_____

· ·

_____

_____

_____

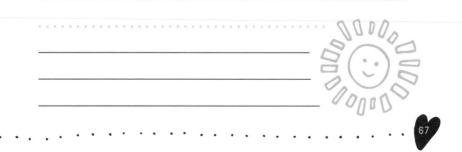

day 118

What makes you sexy is your...

_____

_____

_____

. . . .

_____

_____

_____

day 119

The best sex we ever had was...

_____

_____

_____

. . . .

_____

_____

_____

day 120

My favorite photo of you is the one where you're...

_____

_____

. . . .

_____

_____

day 121

How do you feel about sexting?

_____

_____

_____

. . . .

_____

_____

_____

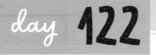

day 122

What's the best kind of foreplay?

_____

_____

_____

. . . .

_____

_____

_____

day 123

Describe one of our most memorable nights together.

_____

_____

. . . .

_____

_____

day 124

What is our next big milestone together? How do you feel about it?

_____

_____

· ·

_____

_____

day 125

How do you feel about living together?

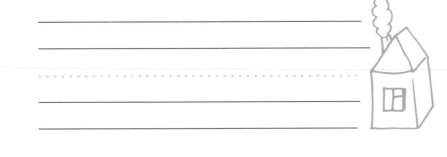

_____

_____

· ·

_____

_____

 **day 126**

What travel dreams do you have for us?

_____

_____

_____

· ·

_____

_____

_____

 **day 127**

How do you feel about the word _forever_?

_____

_____

_____

· ·

_____

_____

_____

day **128**

**What are the ingredients for a
happy, long-lasting marriage?**

day 129

How do you feel about having (more) children together?

_____
_____
_____
· ·
_____
_____
_____

day 130

How many kids is too many kids?

_____
_____
 ·
_____
_____

day 131

If we were to open a business together, what kind would it be?

_____

_____

. . . .

_____

_____

day 132

How can I help you succeed in your job or career?

_____

_____

_____

. . . .

_____

_____

_____

day 133

What do we keep getting better at doing?

_____

_____

_____

. . . .

_____

_____

_____

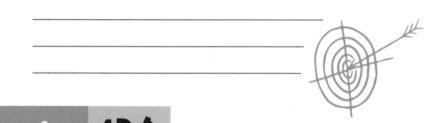

day 134

**How can we bring our families
together in the future?**

_____

_____

. . . .

_____

_____

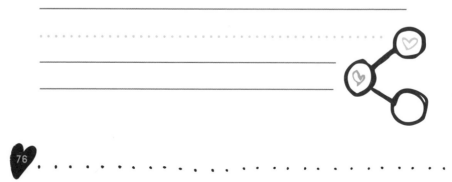

day 135

How can we bring our friends together in the future?

_____

_____

. . . .

_____

_____

day 136

What couples do you hope to get to know better?

_____

_____

. . . .

_____

_____

day 137

What couple do you hope we'll be like in the future?

_____

_____

_____

· ·

_____

_____

_____

day 138

What do you wish for us?

_____

_____

· ·

_____

_____

day 139

What individual goals do you have for yourself?

_____

_____

_____

. . . .

_____

_____

_____

day 140

When is it better to focus on the present?

_____

_____

_____

. . . .

_____

_____

_____

 day **141**

What's one prediction you can confidently make about our future?

_____
_____
· ·
_____
_____

 day **142**

What disagreements about the future do you hope we can resolve?

_____
_____
_____
· ·
_____
_____
_____

day 143

How might our relationship grow the longer we stay together?

_____

_____

. . . .

_____

_____

day 144

What event are you looking forward to attending with me?

_____

_____

. . . .

_____

_____

day 145

What do you look forward to about growing older?

_____
_____
. . . .
_____
_____

day 146

What do you hope will never change?

_____
_____
_____
. . . .
_____
_____
_____

day 147

What do you hope to learn more about?

_____

_____

_____

· ·

_____

_____

_____

day 148

What are you learning to let go of?

_____

_____

_____

· ·

_____

_____

_____

day 149

Describe our future together or draw it here.

_____

_____

_____

. . . .

_____

_____

_____

day 150

How can we help each other stay healthy?

_____

_____

_____

. . . .

_____

_____

_____

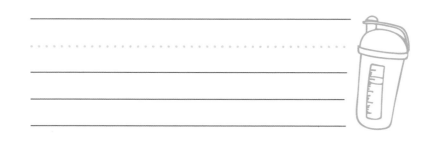

day 151

How comfortable are you with sharing money?

day 152

What should we be saving for together?

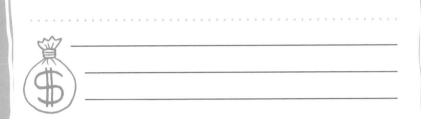

When will we know that we've "made it"?

_____

_____

_____

· ·

_____

_____

_____

Would you rather earn more money or find more satisfying work?

_____

_____

· ·

_____

_____

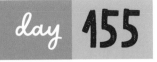

day 155

What job do you think I'd be really good at?

_____

_____

_____

· ·

_____

_____

_____

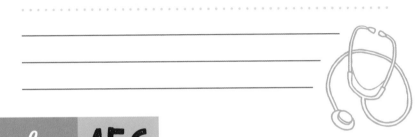

day 156

What do you think will become more important to you in the future?

_____

_____

_____

· ·

_____

_____

_____

day 157

What investments do you think will pay off?

_____

_____

_____

· ·

_____

_____

_____

day 158

What changes do you expect to happen over the next decade?

_____

_____

_____

· ·

_____

_____

_____

day 159

What hobbies do you hope to add to your life?

_____

_____

· ·

_____

_____

day 160

**What do you wish you could
make more time for?**

_____

_____

· ·

_____

_____

What plans are you making for us?

_____

_____

_____

. . . .

_____

_____

_____

day **162**

What would you ask a fortune-teller about us?

_____

_____

. . . .

_____

_____

day 163

How many romantic relationships have you had?

_____

_____

· ·

_____

_____

day 164

Do you think it's good or bad to keep some secrets? Explain why.

_____

_____

· ·

_____

_____

day 165

What's one thing I may not know about your past?

_____

_____

_____

· ·

_____

_____

_____

day 166

When was the last time I pushed your buttons?

_____

_____

_____

· ·

_____

_____

_____

What's the best way for me to make it up to you?

_____

_____

_____

· ·

_____

_____

_____

day **168**

What kind of surprises do you like, if any?

_____

_____

· ·

_____

_____

day **169**

How do you like your birthday to be celebrated?

_____

_____

. . . .

_____

_____

day **170**

What is the most daring thing you've done?

_____

_____

_____

. . . .

_____

_____

_____

day 171

What don't most people know about you?

_____

_____

_____

. . . .

_____

_____

_____

day 172

What more do you wish you knew about me?

_____

_____

_____

. . . .

_____

_____

_____

day 173

What was the last lie you told?

_____

_____

. . . .

_____

_____

day 174

When the bill arrives, I:

☐ ☐   AM HAPPY TO PAY IT

☐ ☐   WOULD LIKE TO SPLIT IT

☐ ☐   DON'T CARE WHO PAYS— WE SHARE MONEY!

☐ ☐   THINK YOU SHOULD PAY MORE

☐ ☐   THINK YOU SHOULD PAY LESS

day 175

If you were tempted to stray, I would want you to...

_____
_____
_____

_____
_____
_____

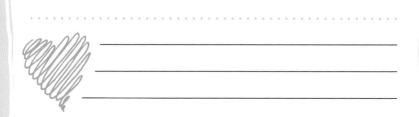

day 176

If I were ever tempted to stray, I would...

_____
_____
_____
_____

day 177

!?

What topic could you go on and on about?

day 178

What makes you feel most vulnerable?

day 179

What makes you feel most alive?

_____

_____

_____

· ·

_____

_____

_____

day 180

What do you wish I would say more often?

_____

_____

_____

· ·

_____

_____

_____

LOVE YOU

day **181**

What do you wish I would do more often?

_____
_____
_____
. . . .
_____
_____
_____

day **182**

Have you ever bragged about me? What did you say?

_____
_____
_____
. . . .
_____
_____
_____

day 183

What would you never tell your friends about us?

_____

_____

· ·

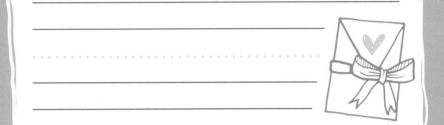

_____

day 184

What do you think your parents think of us?

_____

_____

_____

· ·

_____

_____

_____

day 185

As a team, we're probably best equipped to:

☐ ☐ FIGHT A BEAR

☐ ☐ BATTLE A SHARK

☐ ☐ WRESTLE AN ALLIGATOR

☐ ☐ WE'RE LOVERS, NOT FIGHTERS.

day 186

What are you always excited to do together?

_____

_____

. . . .

_____

_____

 day **187**

What is your worst fear?

_____

_____

_____

· ·

_____

_____

_____

 day **188**

What do you consider your
greatest accomplishment?

_____

_____

_____

· ·

_____

_____

_____

day 189

What do you believe in?

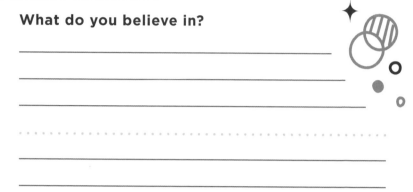

_____

_____

_____

_____

_____

_____

day 190

What are you skeptical about?

_____

_____

_____

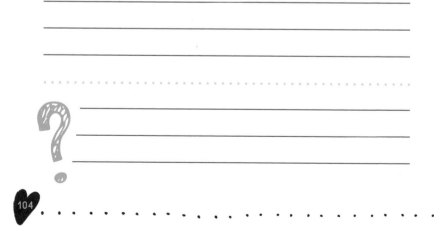

_____

_____

_____

day 191

What were you thinking about the last time we had sex?

_____

_____

. . . .

_____

_____

day 192

Where do you wish we could go right now?

_____

_____

_____

. . . .

_____

_____

_____

Who likes me the most of all your family and friends?

_____

_____

_____

· ·

_____

_____

_____

What flaw of mine do you find endearing?

_____

_____

· ·

_____

_____

day 195

What celebrity do you have a crush on?

_____

_____

_____

. . . .

_____

_____

_____

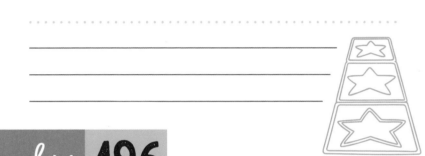

day 196

What was the dumbest thing you ever did?

_____

_____

_____

. . . .

_____

_____

_____

day 197

What was the smartest thing you ever did?

_____

_____

_____

· ·

_____

_____

_____

day 198

If you won the lottery, what would you do with the money?

_____

_____

_____

· ·

_____

_____

_____

Who are you secretly jealous of?

_____
_____
_____
· ·
_____
_____
_____

What were you like as a kid?

_____
_____
· ·
_____
_____

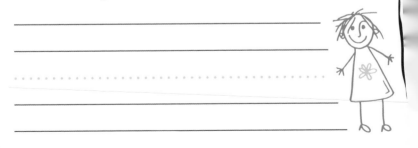

day 201

What were you like as a teenager?

_____

_____

_____

· ·

_____

_____

_____

day 202

Who was your first love?

_____

_____

· ·

_____

_____

day 203

If you got a (new) tattoo, what would it be? Where would you put it?

_____

_____

. . . .

_____

_____

day 204

Which contact or app do you wish you could delete from my phone?

_____

_____

_____

. . . .

_____

_____

_____

day 205

What town or state could you picture us moving to?

_____

_____

· ·

_____

_____

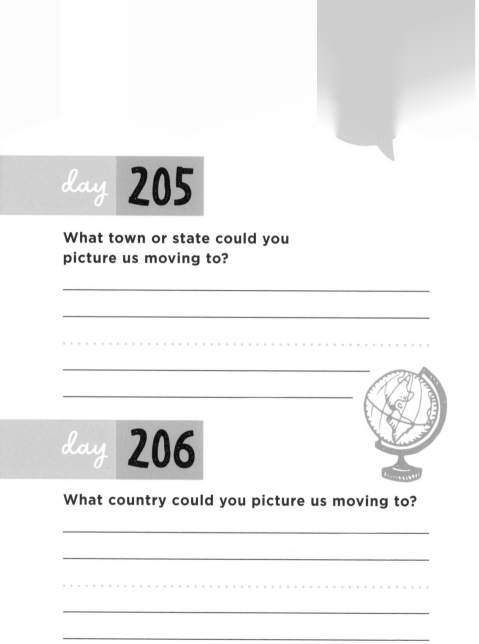

day 206

What country could you picture us moving to?

_____

_____

· ·

_____

_____

day **207**

What class could we take together?

_____

_____

 . . . .

_____

_____

day **208**

What sport could we try together?

_____

_____

_____

. . . .

_____

_____

_____

day **209**

What is the farthest you've ever been from home?

_____

_____

. . . .

_____

_____

day **210**

What makes life an adventure?

_____

_____

_____

. . . .

_____

_____

_____

day **211**

How adventurous would you say you are?

_____

_____

_____

. . . .

_____

_____

_____

day **212**

What have I introduced you to?

_____

_____

_____

. . . .

_____

_____

_____

 *day* **213**

What is a fear we could conquer together?

_____

_____

_____

· ·

_____

_____

_____

 *day* **214**

What new local spot could we try together?

_____

_____

_____

· ·

_____

_____

_____

day 215

What do you think is the most interesting thing about you?

_____

_____

. . . .

_____

_____

day 216

If the world is our playground, where should we play next?

_____

_____

. . . .

_____

_____

day 217

Where do you see us in a year?

_____

_____

_____

. . . .

_____

_____

_____

day 218

Where do you see us in—don't freak out!—a decade?

_____

_____

. . . .

_____

_____

 day **219**

What life change are you most excited about?

 day **220**

How would you define this stage of our relationship?

day 221

If our lives together were a film, what kind of film would you like it to be:

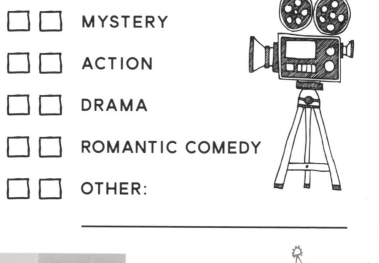

- ☐ ☐ MYSTERY
- ☐ ☐ ACTION
- ☐ ☐ DRAMA
- ☐ ☐ ROMANTIC COMEDY
- ☐ ☐ OTHER:

_____

day 222

When was the last time we threw a party?

_____

_____

. . . .

_____

_____

day 223

What are you most passionate about?

_____

_____

_____

· ·

_____

_____

_____

day 224

When was the last time we had a good laugh?

_____

_____

· ·

_____

_____

day 225

If you could pick a new name for yourself, what would it be?

_____

_____

. . . .

_____

_____

day 226

If we were a celebrity couple, what would people call us?

_____

_____

. . . .

_____

_____

 122

What actions or characteristics define us as a couple?

_____

_____

_____

· ·

_____

_____

_____

day **228**

What is your idea of a good time?

_____

_____

_____

· ·

_____

_____

_____

day

**What fun change could we make
to our life together?**

_____

_____

_____

· ·

_____

_____

_____

day

What makes you feel like a kid again?

_____

_____

_____

· ·

_____

_____

_____

day 231

What makes you fall in love with me all over again?

_____
_____
. . . .
_____
_____

day 232

Where is your (or our) happy place?

_____
_____
_____
. . . .
_____
_____
_____

day 233

When have we taken a leap of faith together?

_____
_____
_____

· ·

_____

_____

_____

day **234**

What is one item on both of our bucket lists?

_____
_____

· ·

_____
_____

day 235

What's your idea of a fun night out:

- [ ] [ ] PUB TRIVIA
- [ ] [ ] DINNER AT A NICE RESTAURANT
- [ ] [ ] DINNER PARTY AT A FRIEND'S
- [ ] [ ] MOVIE THEATER
- [ ] [ ] SPORTING EVENT
- [ ] [ ] HOME IS WHERE MY HEART IS.

day 236

What has worked to spice up our sex life?

_____

_____

. . . .

_____

_____

day 237

What does your heart want today?

_____

_____

_____

· ·

_____

_____

_____

day 238

What does your body want today?

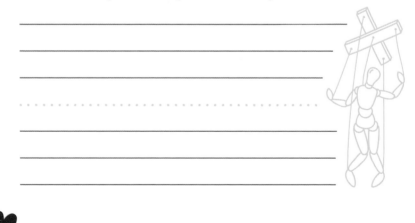

_____

_____

_____

· ·

_____

_____

_____

Where would you be most excited to have sex:

☐ ☐ IN THE WOODS

☐ ☐ IN THE BACK SEAT OF A CAR

☐ ☐ ON A BEACH

☐ ☐ ON OUR KITCHEN TABLE

☐ ☐ IN A NICE HOTEL ROOM

☐ ☐ IN OUR BEDROOM, THANK YOU VERY MUCH!

☐ ☐ OTHER:

_____

day 240

Whose family is weirder?

_____

_____

· ·

_____

_____

day 241

Which of us is funnier?

_____

_____

_____

· ·

_____

_____

_____

day **242**

Which of us is more introverted?

day **243**

Which of us is more likely to get arrested? Why?

day 244

Who's more likely to become famous? For what?

_____

_____

· ·

_____

_____

day 245

Whose response to danger is fight, and whose is flight?

_____

_____

· ·

_____

_____

day 246

Who is a better driver?

_____

_____

_____

· ·

_____

_____

_____

day 247

Who is a better cook?

_____

_____

_____

· ·

_____

_____

_____

day 248

Who is better with money?

day 249

Who is more competitive?

day 250

Who is a better dancer?

day 251

Who is a better singer?

day 252

Who is usually the first to say *I'm sorry*?

day 253

Which of us is neater?

 **day 254**

Which of us is more fashionable?

_____
_____
_____
. . . .
_____
_____
_____

 **day 255**

Which of us is harder to read?

_____
_____
_____
. . . .
_____
_____
_____

day 256

Which of us is more romantic?

_____

_____

_____

. . . .

_____

_____

_____

day 257

Which of us is more likely to win on _Jeopardy!_?

_____

_____

_____

. . . .

_____

_____

_____

day **258**

Which of us is more of a planner?

_____

_____

_____

. . . .

_____

_____

_____

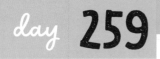

day **259**

Which of us is more creative?

_____

_____

. . . .

_____

_____

day 260

Which of us is more of an optimist?

_____

_____

_____

_____

. . . .

_____

_____

_____

day 261

Who would have a harder time giving up their cell phone for a week?

_____

_____

. . . .

_____

_____

day 262

Who tends to get the TV remote?

_____

_____

_____

. . . .

_____

_____

_____

day 263

How are we the perfect balance?

_____

_____

_____

. . . .

_____

_____

_____

 264

What beliefs are you glad we share?

_____

_____

. . . .

_____

_____

 265

What values did you grow up with?

_____

_____

_____

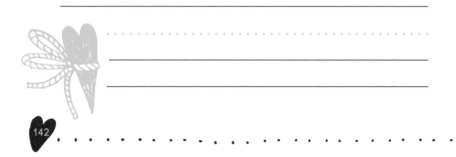

. . . .

_____

_____

day 266

What do we value most as a couple?

_____

_____

. . . .

_____

_____

day 267

When have we put each other first?

_____

_____

_____

. . . .

_____

_____

_____

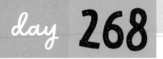

day 268

**When have we had to make a
difficult decision together?**

_____

_____

· ·

_____

_____

day 269

The secret to making this relationship work is...

_____

_____

· ·

_____

_____

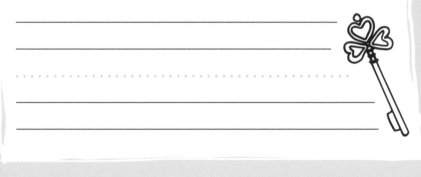

 day **270**

What are your top three priorities?

_____

_____

_____

· ·

_____

_____

_____

 day **271**

How do you like to be taken care of when you're sick?

_____

_____

· ·

_____

_____

day 272

How should I talk to you when you're angry?

_____

_____

_____

· ·

_____

_____

_____

day 273

What's the best thing I could say or do when you are sad?

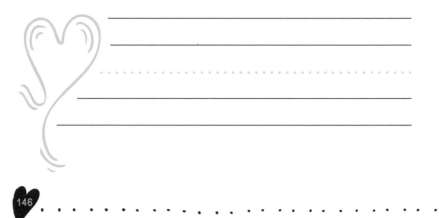

_____

_____

· ·

_____

_____

day 274

How would you fill in this blank: The couple who _____ together, stays together.

_____

_____

· ·

_____

_____

day 275

What are the red flags you look out for in a relationship?

_____

_____

· ·

_____

_____

day 276

Two people we should try to set up are...

_____

_____

. . . .

_____

_____

day 277

When have you needed more alone time?

_____

_____

_____

. . . .

_____

_____

_____

day 278

When have you needed more couple time?

_____

_____

_____

· ·

_____

_____

_____

day 279

What does it mean to be a good partner?

_____

_____

_____

· ·

_____

_____

_____

day 280

What does it mean to be a good son or daughter?

_____

_____

. . . .

_____

_____

day 281

What does it mean to be a good parent?

_____

_____

_____

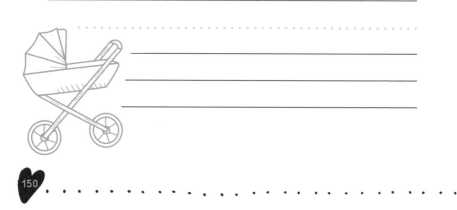

. . . .

_____

_____

_____

day 282

How can we help others in our lives?

_____

_____

. . . .

_____

_____

day 283

What difference do you hope you can make in the world?

_____

_____

. . . .

_____

_____

day 284

Something I love about your family is...

_____

_____

_____

· ·

_____

_____

_____

day 285

Something I love about your best friend is...

_____

_____

· ·

_____

_____

 day **286**

You were there for me when...

_____

_____

_____

· ·

_____

_____

_____

 day **287**

We don't need money to...

_____

_____

_____

· ·

_____

_____

_____

**You don't have to be perfect
for me. It's okay if you...**

_____

_____

· ·

_____

_____

When I've had a bad day, you're there to...

_____

_____

_____

· ·

_____

_____

_____

day 290

The most helpful advice I could give to a new couple is...

_____

_____

· ·

_____

_____

day 291

When you're away, I miss your...

_____

_____

_____

· ·

_____

_____

day 292

Some of the big plans I have for us include...

_____

_____

_____

· ·

_____

_____

_____

day 293

**What daily ritual would be fun
to add to our lives?**

_____

_____

· ·

_____

_____

day 294

Let's not let the little things get
in the way. By that I mean...

_____

_____

_____

· ·

_____

_____

_____

day 295

I have so much respect for the way you...

_____

_____

_____

· ·

_____

_____

_____

day 296

It's important to tell the truth, even when...

_____

_____

_____

. . . .

_____

_____

_____

day 297

If I had to write a vow to you
right now, it would be...

_____

_____

. . . .

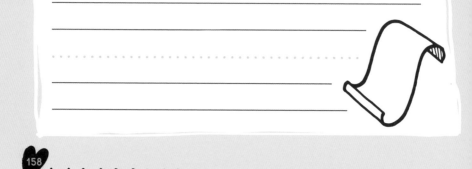

_____

day 298

You're the only person in the world who...

_____

_____

· ·

_____

_____

day 299

How are we stronger together?

_____

_____

· ·

_____

_____

day **300**

If we had a motto as a couple, what would it be?

_____

_____

_____

· ·

_____

_____

_____

day **301**

You make me feel seen when you...

_____

_____

_____

· ·

_____

_____

_____

day 302

What is the best way to protect our relationship?

_____

_____

. . . .

_____

_____

day 303

I'm proud of the way we...

_____

_____

_____

. . . .

_____

_____

_____

day 304

Someone we'll learn to...

_____

_____

_____

· · · · · · · · · · · · · · · · · ·

_____

_____

_____

day 305

I was never more sure of our bond than when we...

_____

_____

· · · · · · · · · · · · · · · · · ·

_____

_____

day **306**

We deserve a trophy for...

_____

_____

_____

_____

_____

_____

day **307**

What advice have we been given as a couple? Did we take it?

_____

_____

_____

_____

_____

_____

day 308

People who have guided our relationship include:

_____

_____

. . . .

_____

_____

day 309

If there's anything we need more of in our relationship, it's...

_____

_____

_____

. . . .

_____

_____

_____

day 310

A time when you've gone the extra mile to make me happy was...

_____

_____

. . . .

_____

_____

day 311

WINNER

We are a winning combination of...

_____

_____

_____

. . . .

_____

_____

_____

day 312

What is something we haven't had to face yet?

_____

_____

_____

. . . .

_____

_____

_____

day 313

How has our relationship been tested?

_____

_____

. . . .

_____

_____

day **314**

**We have built our relationship
on a foundation of...**

_____

_____

_____

. . . .

_____

_____

_____

day **315**

Our parents should be proud of how we...

_____

_____

_____

. . . .

_____

_____

_____

day 316

We should always make time to...

_____

_____

_____

. . . .

_____

_____

_____

day 317

We're lucky because...

_____

_____

_____

. . . .

_____

_____

_____

day 318

How have you changed since first meeting me?

_____
_____
_____
. . . .
_____
_____
_____

day 319

How do you think I've changed?

_____
_____
. . . .
_____
_____

What kind of legacy do
you hope to leave?

_____

_____

. . . .

_____

_____

If someone were to build a monument to
our relationship, what would it look like?

_____

_____

. . . .

_____

_____

 day **322**

I need you in my life because...

_____

_____

_____

· ·

_____

_____

_____

 day **323**

I want you in my life because...

_____

_____

_____

· ·

_____

_____

_____

day 324

The biggest turning point in our relationship was...

_____

_____

_____

. . . .

_____

_____

day 325

A risk I'd be willing to take for you is...

_____

_____

_____

. . . .

_____

_____

day 326

The photo of us that we should enlarge into a giant poster is...

_____

_____

. . . .

_____

_____

day 327

Let's make a promise that we'll never...

_____

_____

_____

. . . .

_____

_____

_____

If we had a chance to begin again, I'd make sure...

_____

_____

· ·

_____

_____

Something we're ready to face together is...

_____

_____

_____

· ·

_____

_____

_____

day 330

This is how far I like to think ahead:

 A DAY

□ □ A WEEK

□ □ A MONTH

□ □ A DECADE OR MORE

□ □ I'M LIVING IN THE NOW

day 331

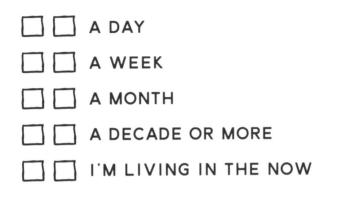

If we were to invent a holiday just for us, it would be...

_____

_____

_____

_____

_____

_____

 day **332**

When we're old and gray...

_____
_____
_____
· ·
_____
_____
_____

 day **333**

If someone at our favorite restaurant
named a dish after us, it would be called:

_____
_____
_____
· ·
_____
_____
_____

day **334**

My main worries about the future are...

_____

_____

_____

· ·

_____

_____

_____

day **335**

What possibilities excite you?

_____

_____

· ·

_____

_____

day  **336**

Who do we want in our inner circle for the rest of our lives?

_____

_____

. . . .

_____

_____

day  **337**

What books or movies shaped your ideas about love?

_____

_____

. . . .

_____

_____

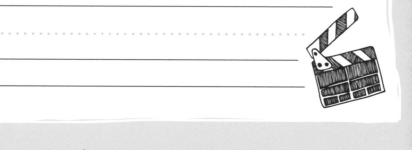

day **338**

One thing I never worry about is...

_____

_____

_____

· ·

_____

_____

_____

day **339**

What do you love sharing with me?

_____

_____

_____

· ·

_____

_____

_____

day

What is the spice of life, in your opinion?

_____

_____

_____

. . . .

_____

_____

_____

day

What are you most grateful for?

_____

_____

_____

. . . .

_____

_____

_____

How old do you feel?

_____
_____
. . . .
_____
_____

Here's how you're adorable at any age:

_____
_____
_____
. . . .
_____
_____
_____

day **344**

**What holiday do you most love
spending with me?**

_____

_____

· ·

_____

_____

day **345**

What new tradition could we start?

_____

_____

_____

· ·

_____

_____

_____

 day **346**

What are the unspoken rules
of our relationship?

_____

_____

· ·

_____

_____

 day **347**

How much money do we need
to live a good life?

_____

_____

_____

· ·

_____

_____

_____

day 348

How could we reenact our first date today?

_____

_____

_____

· ·

_____

_____

_____

day 349

**Here's one technological advancement
that could help our relationship:**

_____

_____

_____

· ·

_____

_____

_____

day **350**

The best gift you ever got me was...

_____

_____

· ·

_____

_____

day **351**

Here's what we should put in
a time capsule of us:

_____

_____

_____

· ·

_____

_____

_____

day 352

What real-life experience could we turn into a best seller?

_____
_____
. . . .
_____
_____

day 353

If we were superheroes, who would be our archnemesis?

_____
_____
. . . .
_____
_____

day 354

The way to your heart seems to be through your...

_____

_____

_____

· ·

_____

_____

_____

day 355

What's weird about the two of us?

_____

_____

· ·

_____

_____

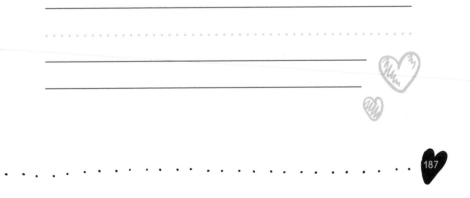

 **day 356**

Here's one little way I like to show my love...

_____

_____

_____

· ·

_____

_____

_____

 **day 357**

What's the best way to celebrate
our anniversary?

_____

_____

_____

· ·

_____

_____

_____

day 358

Here's why our sex life will always stay exciting:

_____

_____

· ·

_____

_____

day 359

What does success look like for you?

_____

_____

_____

· ·

_____

_____

_____   SUCCESS

day 360

Something people don't appreciate enough about you is...

_____
_____
. . . .
_____
_____

day 361

This is what I daydream about:

_____
_____
_____
. . . .
_____
_____
_____

day 362

The best way to head off into
the sunset together is:

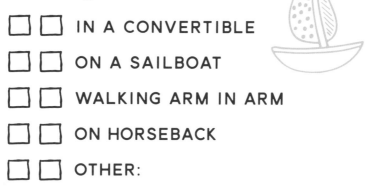

- ☐ ☐ IN A CONVERTIBLE
- ☐ ☐ ON A SAILBOAT
- ☐ ☐ WALKING ARM IN ARM
- ☐ ☐ ON HORSEBACK
- ☐ ☐ OTHER:

_____

day 363

One day we'll look back on
this moment and think...

_____

_____

. . . .

_____

_____

day 364

I'm glad you're by my side because...

_____

_____

_____

· ·

_____

_____

_____

day 365

This year together as a couple has been...

_____

_____

_____

· ·

_____

_____

_____